Addict

Cherie Shanko

Presentation by *BookLeaf Publishing*

Web: www.bookleafpub.com

E-mail: info@bookleafpub.com

ISBN: 9789357693035

First edition 2023

Letting go

We all seek to escape something
Yet we cannot outrun our past.
Our only hope lives in accepting life as it is.;
letting go of a life once lived to meet
the one we have yet to know.
If you can do that, the peace you seek
will follow.

My world has ended many times
just to begin again.
And the bravest thing I ever did was
continuing to live when I wanted to die.
Just for today hope wins.
It's easy to love the nice things about myself

but embracing the hellish parts
Is where the grandest,

the most daring adventure begins.
If I am going to make it on this earth,
I best begin this journey.

DOC

Sometimes life isn't about living,
There's not always that luxury.
Some of us just need to survive.
In our own way, we are all addicts
just struggling with our own drug of choice.
Searching for our fix.

Fresh wounds

Maybe there's a *little* bit of insanity in
pretending that my wounds don't hurt;
Putting on a brave face, I press on my
most recent bruise to get used to the pain
And it all becomes numb.

Beautiful armor

Masks are magic and mystery crafted by our trauma.
Each piece is delicately picked for the part we begin to play.And the longer we wear the mask, the harder it is to remove.

After a while, will I stop recognizing the person in the mirror?

Hibernation

Her leaves too had fallen.
Once a colorful parade of praise
was now simply bare bark.
And she was left to decide
Was this the end or just the beginning?

Fortress

When childhood dreams fade away
And nightmares take their place
is it just a part of growing up
or meeting monsters face to face.

So I built a tower to keep me safe
A fortress for my own
But the monsters never lived outside
This fortress is their home.

A cure for living

A sickness lives inside of me that no medicine can cure. Progressive, chronic, fatal. Whether it's a disease or a flaw in my morality,the treatment is all the same by those who don't understand because they cannot see the broken soul, the lost dreams, the desperation in my eyes. They don't know how this disease grows with each targeted word they say aimed to hurt, each unmet expectation, each rejection of who I am, and each time I say goodbye knowing I may never see you again.

It's a lonely kind of sickness and all I can do is treat the pain with the same poison that made me sick. Rinse and repeat.

The company of misery

It's true that not all misery prefers company.
Some misery prefers the dark and haunted hours
where only the moon dares to show its face..
And the ghosts of my past tear into my sanity
until all my demons are set free.
I always find you there.

Lonely

Lonely is the stale AC air
I inhale on sleepless nights
when my thoughts create half-truths
convinced of your heroism
and desperation becomes the boogie man
making me believe I need to be rescued.

Moving on

Moving on means no longer sleeping by the
door listening for your key in the lock.
It's climbing each step up to the bedroom, afraid
of what awaits me, but pretending it doesn't
bother me anymore. Where finding a mountain
of pillows lingering with the scent of you,
doesn't remind me of nights we spent in love. I
stay to my side not daring to touch the pain that
lives in the emptiness of your half. But when I
close my eyes I cannot help finding comfort in
the blankets wrapped tightly around me like
your arms as you used to. And before I fall
asleep, I always open the window and wait for
the familiar brush of air that dances across my
neck like your slumbered breath once did.

You may be gone, but your ghost remains.

Burning

I see the pain in your eyes as you look at the
flaming edges of our fractured future and the
box of matches in my hand.

In the way you listen for the asterisks in my
sentences expecting details to have gotten lost
along the way.

In the scent of our dinner grown cold on your
plate for the lump in your throat was too great to
be bested.

In the taste of the tears falling slowly from your
eyes when you can no longer hold them back.

In the cautious embraces we now take
as if my touch would cause you to unravel.

If love and pain come in equal parts.
I know how deeply you hurt because I knew
how strongly you loved.

Devil in Disguise

It gave me a sense of peace that's beyond words.
I cradled in a gentle warmth that felt like home
and I drank every drop of that euphoric moment.
Life had no worries and I was untouchable.
This was the greatest love of my life.
I craved its soothing touch and I prayed
it would always be near.

Then it was gone and it's like the world ended.
Desperation felt like oxygen I could not breathe
and my heart bore a hole that could not be filled.
I abandoned my own life in search of what it
promised so many years ago.
Because I loved it with everything I had
that left me with no room to love myself.

XXIV

I count the days in tally marks testifying to the
24 hours gone by where each stroke of the pen
reminds me of the battle I have just won.
And though others may see the wreckage, they
cannot truly know the price of the fight or the
full-bodied cry for salvation that lives right
below the surface of my best poker face.
My soul is a tattered battlefield from days I was
not strong enough to face the person I have
become.

Butterfly Wings

When you see a butterfly do you marvel at the beauty displayed on their perfectly painted wings as they quickly flutter by or do you stand in amazement at the transformation it had to go through in order to fly?

Healing

I know it seems confusing
that I ask for understanding
when you were just collateral damage
in a war I was waging against myself.

But this IS healing.

Each victory may look like nothing
More than a rainy Sunday afternoon.

But that rain is the sweetest rain I have ever
tasted and on the most beautiful afternoon.

At last, I'm free to enjoy the simple things.

After

hen we feel we're broken
and that we can't go on.
It'll be our leap of faith
that proves that we are strong.

Look for the wins and not the loss
in these battles that we fight.
This is a war that's from within
And only you can dim your light.

Just for today, do the next right thing
With no promise of tomorrow
Because If we work this step by step
Peace will replace sorrow.

Fellowship

They were just ordinary people,
but they were my miracles.
For they have seen the most of me
and they have chosen to stay.
While the world demands beauty,
they fell in love with my scars.

And I, in turn, had fallen in love
with them and their strange world.
They have become well-tangled in my soul.

A Life Worth Living

I live for ordinary days.
For the Monday through Friday grind
which allows me to chase my dreams.
For the birthday parties and balloons,
and the sweet taste of a life I still get to live.
For the bedtime stories and goodnight kisses
after evening strolls on chilly nights

underneath a star-covered sky.
For the thank you's given generously and
the apologies said in earnest.
For the sunshine that starts each day without fail.
For me, these are the things that matter most.

Light

I looked at her
as she looked at the sky
and even the stars were jealous
of how bright she could shine.
For on the darkest of nights
her light only grows.

Love thyself

Self-love is the ultimate act of kindness. It's a journey of getting to know who you are, as you are, with an open heart and gentlest hands.

But loving ourselves is a difficult feat. Because who are we to accept love knowing our flaws, our shame, our failed attempts at being a success, our too-wide waistline, our broken hearts, our bad days, and our deepest regrets?

Loving one's self means seeing yourself for the human you are and all the many magical things that make you unique. We were never meant to be perfect. So give compassion to your mistakes and forgiveness to your follies. Allow yourself the privilege of feeling proud of things done well and moments you were a total badass.

You are a love story just waiting to be told.

Home

A home tells the story of who you are and what
you love.

It is here you grow up and grow old.
Where you plant roots and watch them grow.
Where gathered friends and family fill the rooms
with love and laughter.

At home, the light is always on
and loving arms are never far.

A home is more than the walls that hold it up.
It is a feeling, a place of belonging, and a sense
of security.
It is built on faith and generosity, and furnished
with precious memories.

I think, at last, I have found mine.

www.ingramcontent.com/pod-product-compliance
Lightning Source LLC
LaVergne TN
LVHW050309200726
843509LV00015B/3240